# A Life Emerging

# A Life Emerging

*A Poetic Journey Out of Depression*

## ELÁN YARDENA

iUniverse, Inc.
Bloomington

A Life Emerging
A Poetic Journey Out of Depression

iUniverse books may be ordered through booksellers or by contacting:

iUniverse
1663 Liberty Drive
Bloomington, IN 47403
www.iuniverse.com
1-800-Authors (1-800-288-4677)

ISBN: 978-1-4620-5841-9 (sc)
ISBN: 978-1-4620-5842-6 (hc)
ISBN: 978-1-4620-5843-3 (ebk)

Library of Congress Control Number: 2011918448

Printed in the United States of America

iUniverse rev. date: 10/25/2011

For my three wonderful children, who always give my life purpose and allow me to experience the joy of giving and receiving unconditional love.

# PREFACE

Three years ago, I found myself struggling with depression again, a problem I had battled for more than three decades. The depression was very intense, and interfered with my work. The first time I met with William Brad Brager, MA, LPC, to decide if he could help me, I wasn't hopeful, just desperate. Over those three decades, I had seen many therapists, counselors, and psychologists. Some helped me identify issues, needs, and destructive mindsets, but none ever offered any real, tangible solutions. Unfortunately, the therapy process usually took months to cover all the trauma and abuse I had experienced before we got to core issues. It was a painful, exhausting, and costly process, which ended in my concluding that therapy could not help. The fear of going through all that again prevented me from seeking help for a long time. I thought I would have to deal with depression forever; the most I could expect was occasional help in lessening its effects.

I decided to speed up the process with Brad by clearly spelling out my impossible expectations in our initial session: I wanted to end depression for good, and find happiness and contentment. After giving him a synopsis of what I knew and where I wanted to be, I asked him directly if he could help me get there. To my complete surprise, he said yes. Still skeptical, I asked him for his plan to achieve that. I wanted to know if his was an empty promise or if there was substance behind it. As he began to describe what some of my current obstacles were, I realized he was the first person to really understand me and actually know what to do about my depression.

His process did not require me to go back through all the past garbage. Instead, the focus was on addressing the here and now. If events in the present brought back something from the past, we would handle it in a less invasive way, with gentleness and compassion. Ultimately, it was Brad's confidence that I could do it that made me decide to begin this process again. I could not have imagined what an amazing transformation would occur in such a short time.

His therapeutic plan started with working on daily mental dialogues: those internal tape recordings we use to torture ourselves. Decreasing emotional reactions came through learning and practice, *mindfulness meditation*, and becoming more aware of the *cognitive narrative experience* (what we tell ourselves). Though mindfulness meditation is rooted in Buddhism, many areas of psychotherapy use it. It teaches stepping back to observe thoughts and emotions as passing events conditioned by previous experiences. By my learning to remain aware of but not controlled by my reactions, the *automatic cognitive-affective spirals* that can lead to depression lose their power.

As a Christian, I informed him I was open to seeing what mindfulness meditation offered, but that if it conflicted with my beliefs, I would quit. It is funny how desperation helps us lay down our prejudices against other philosophies and religions. There was a time when I would not have given a notion rooted in Buddhism a fair hearing.

Brad recommended several books, knowing I was an avid reader. After reading Jon Kabat-Zinn's *Full Catastrophe Living* and *Wherever You Go There You Are*, I came to several conclusions. First, I found nothing conflicting with my Christian beliefs. In fact, the material in Kabat-Zinn's book was completely in line with much of Old Testament and New Testament cultures even if very different from modern Christianity. Second, I determined that the primary premise was that by learning to stay in the present moment rather than reliving the trauma of the past or worrying about the future, one could actually find peace of mind and contentment. Wow! This offered a way to stop most of the suffering I inflicted upon myself. It meant taking personal responsibility for my own choices and not playing the blame game.

The third conclusion was that mindfulness meditation offered empowerment to control impulses and lifelong habit patterns of reacting to experiences. The prolonged times of silent awareness in mindfulness meditation, time apart from my normally hectic routine, teaches this self-restraint.

Eventually I felt I needed practical instruction in meditation. So I began meditation lessons with Micki Fine, who had trained with Jon Kabat-Zinn in Massachusetts. She had practiced mindfulness meditation for over twenty years and taught it since 1995. While the lessons were helpful, it was the full-day workshops in silent meditation and the weekend silent retreats where most of my breakthroughs happened.

Within a few weeks of beginning the therapy process with Brad, the poetry began to form in my mind. I always kept journals, but nothing seemed clear enough to write about using full sentences and narrative form. I was not trying to write poetry with commercial value. I just wanted to get confused thoughts and feelings out in the open to deal with them. It was not until over two years had passed that I found my own unique poetic voice and style.

This poetry allowed me to express myself more clearly. It often revealed things my normal self-protection mechanisms sought to hide. There is no one-size-fits-all formula for self-knowledge through poetry. Everyone needs to willingly embark on that journey of self-discovery and healing in their own unique way. Additional resources for getting started are available in the back of this book.

# ACKNOWLEDGMENTS

There is no way I can ever thank W. Brad Brager and Micki Fine enough for showing me how to find my life.

It is an understatement that attending Lakewood Church weekly and being encouraged by Joel Osteen's timely messages often gave me a focus for the next week, which was critical for maintaining equilibrium and keeping depression at bay. Even when traveling, I watch the live streaming service online.

A special thanks to Robin Davidson, PhD, Associate Professor at University of Houston-Downtown, for her encouragement and expertise when I came for my first poetry lesson.

The Jung Center of Houston and Spirit Rock Meditation Center in California were essential to my learning. These centers offer, through retreats and workshops, a wide variety of opportunities that empower people to become their best selves. Every event I attended at both centers brought a new epiphany.

# CONTENTS

# INTRODUCTION

I wrote this book under a pseudonym due to the very personal and transparent nature of its content. I hope that those people mentioned within these poems (not by name, but by relationship) will not suffer by also remaining anonymous. I do not believe using a pseudonym detracts from the message I wish to bring: that there is hope for people struggling with depression or other mental anguish. I hope these poems awaken in others a desire to find healing and health. I also believe that my suffering is similar to the suffering of others who may not be able to articulate their thoughts and feelings yet, but may find their own feelings expressed in these poems.

I do offer some disclaimers. First, this is not a literal reporting of facts. Poetry, in its very essence, is a creative process, which expresses the deepest emotions and thoughts of its author. There is a completely subjective and imaginative aspect to poetry. As with other types of art, the significance of poetry lies in what a poem means to the author and to each reader personally. I fill my poems with imagery and metaphors because that is how I understand life. The poems are completely *phenomenological*: my subjective perspective alone is represented.

Many poems involve family or friends, and their recollections of the events in question may differ from my own. That is fine, because this book is not about them. It is about how my experiences affected me emotionally and psychologically, and how I am resolving those feelings. There might be a certain amount of untruth or unreality in these poems, if one were to view the circumstances objectively. However, we never go through our life experiences objectively. They filter through our prior experiences, *schemas*, personalities, expectations, and even our skewed abilities to see our own and others' intentions. The starting point has to be the original experience, with all its pain, unreality, and imperfection.

Finally, some are uncomfortable with what Jung calls "*the shadow*," that part of us which represents our dark, forbidden, unwanted, and socially feared or unacceptable traits, thoughts, emotions, and behaviors. I wrote many of these poems while I was depressed. While they speak of death as a way out of pain, there was never any intention of acting on those thoughts. I have my children to thank for that. I would never want them to go through what I did when my mother committed suicide. It took a long time for me to let my shadow show, and even longer to accept it so I could be whole. Brad would say that part of his job is to be an example of not being judgmental or critical when the shameful parts of his clients' psyches are expressed. He helped me to stop denying these feelings, and even though that did not mean indulging them either, learning how to stop kicking myself has been essential to stopping so much self-inflicted mental anguish.

# The Issue of Depression

Admitting a problem with depression no longer holds the stigma it did a few decades ago. Attending therapy is no longer an admission of insanity or abnormality. Many recognize the value of professional help in working out relationships, learning to handle mental illness, or dealing with everyday stress and anxiety. Therapy is now normal and often encouraged by family and friends, and even paid for by employers.

The word "depression," however, has become so commonplace that it can represent everything from disappointment or frustration to much more serious emotional feelings, as was the case when Andrea Yates murdered her children while suffering from *post-partum depression*. When someone says that they are depressed, it is not always clear what they mean. For me, depression was something I always remember my mother having in varying degrees. Often I found her crying for days, or silently staring off into space for hours. Before I was a teenager, she committed suicide. I never knew whether my own struggles were inherited genetically, learned through living with her, or a little bit of both. No matter the cause, for me depression has been a lifelong battle.

Growing up with abuse seemed to be a contributing factor for my depression. There was never an apparent way to resolve trauma completely. Bad memories and feelings were locked away somewhere, and every so often they would resurface with all the original pain. Trauma would then be put back in that closet in the back of the mind, unresolved and unchanged, waiting for its next appearance. There was also new trauma and suffering growing out of destructive patterns learned in childhood. Brad said that my resisting change indicated that I had not learned how to challenge some belief learned previously. When I learned to see those beliefs as habits, not absolute truths, my reality changed. I learned that thoughts and emotions are impermanent and influenced by previous conditioning. This greatly lessened their power to affect me.

Over the last forty years, I have read many books, obtained two psychology degrees, and seen many therapists in attempts to find answers. Some therapists were useless. Some were a little helpful, but didn't permanently solve my problems. There are so many different variables playing a part in our problems: family background, parent/family/friend modeling, experiences, personality, motivations, interpretation of circumstances, cultures, resources we have access to, the amount of social pressure to be a certain way, and on and on. This diversity of complications makes for a challenge for therapists and patients.

Finding the right therapy reminds me of the vast number of diets on the market. Every diet offers multiple testimonials of people who miraculously lost weight in record time. But the vast majority of people trying any particular diet fail. Maybe to lose weight or to get rid of depression, a person has to have a customized, completely unique, and personal plan that fits perfectly with the particular set of variables in their life. Looking back over the last three years, I realize that I found a process that fit me perfectly. I believe others can find their perfect process as well.

## The Process

The first part of this process was reevaluating preconceptions, values, beliefs, and behaviors to find truth and sift out lies. Most of my life, I dogmatically held onto ideals, which caused much of my suffering. Most were religious, and therefore more powerful, as I thought they were God's will. It took years to see that I was the only one who could heal me. I had to take responsibility to improve my quality of life, and accept that I was responsible for some of the trauma I had experienced. I always had choices, even if I did not see them or exercise them. I had to stay open to truth, even if it challenged everything I believed or thought I knew.

The second important part of this process was working with the right people. A friend of mine grew up playing competitive sports. He loves it when a coach pushes him beyond his limits. I prefer to learn my options and make my own decisions. Pushing feels like manipulation. I do like a challenge and want the truth, even if it hurts. Brad's style allowed me to go as fast or slow as I needed. He challenged me, but allowed me to follow my own course. He modeled an accepting attitude toward whatever thoughts or emotions we discussed. This gave me a chance to experience acceptance on a new level. Brad's methods were a perfect fit for my personality, needs, and motivations. While I am always open to his insight and advice, I may or may not agree with him or take his recommendations. His willingness to give me that freedom was both refreshing and empowering. I am grateful he could adapt his style for my needs. There are many other styles: simple listener, or more like that coach. Everyone should find the therapist relationship that is right for them.

Another person that made a significant difference for me was my mindfulness meditation teacher, Micki Fine. Her consistent teaching and modeling of acceptance and peace of mind helped greatly. Her gentle reminders to accept my thoughts and emotions without drama were revolutionary on many levels. I think what I appreciated most though was her compassion toward all who suffer.

The most powerful tool Micki taught me involved going back to the point in time that a particular trauma occurred. I could rework the situation with myself as a third party, giving my younger self the compassion, strength, or encouragement she never received. Thich Nhat Hanh describes this process in his book, *Reconciliation: Healing the Inner Child*. I describe my first time in the poem "Save the Child." It healed a very painful memory completely and gave me unbelievable hope that all of this was really working. Several other poems are a direct result of that process, namely "The First Brick," "Strongholds," "Compassion Within," and "Self-Forgiveness." Now, when I recall traumatic events, there is no longer pain. Meditation and therapy replaced the painful memories with a painless version. There is no longer suffering or regret, because I created a new memory of the event. For me, this is true resolution.

The therapy sessions laid the necessary foundation for all of this. It was through our talks that I understood my thoughts and emotions and how I had misinterpreted or internalized them. Once identified, we reevaluated these issues. I was able to change the past and break old patterns rather than reenacting them again. Mindfulness meditation enhanced my self-awareness about thoughts and emotions through training me to focus on my breathing as an anchor.

The third part of the process was learning to write poetry straight from my heart. For me, writing and poetry have always been my way of processing conflict. I maintain a private journal and write down what I am thinking and feeling, even if those sentiments do not make sense. This helps me get emotion out of my head and down on paper, where I can see all the moving parts. Eventually patterns emerge and I start to see what is really going on.

Normally, my poems begin at the point where I see a theme or pattern, covering two to three lines for a start. Just as I finish writing the first lines, the next come to me. I write these, and the next words come. Once the process starts, I typically write until a poem is finished. Some poems take twenty minutes, others a couple days. Occasionally I start a poem and only write a few lines before I am stuck. This means I am not ready yet. I put the lines aside until later when the rest comes to me.

When I reread a finished poem, I am always amazed. The process of writing the poem is actually the process drawing out of my subconscious the explanation of what is going on, as well as a solution or resolution. I read each poem to Brad (and some to Micki). My poems give them a clearer understanding of my mental or emotional processes. It is amazing how much writing reveals of what we hide in conversations. Brad frequently says that I need to reread each poem and listen to the advice it has to offer. He helped me see what much of my poetry meant. The lessons in my poetry were unique, personal recommendations from my own subconscious.

> *What better solution is there than the one created by your own*
> *subconscious, where all your memories and experiences are stored?*
> *Who could know better than yourself exactly what you need?*

The best result of therapy is understanding that I do not have to wait for someone else or be dependent on anything other than my own initiative and willingness to face issues. This takes away the victim mentality, as well as any need to blame others or be resentful.

An additional benefit of poetry over just journaling is that a poem is a piece of art with a beginning, middle, climax, and conclusion. It puts my experience into a finished piece with a title. Habits and thought patterns are hard to break. I often reverted to those I already knew were destructive and depressive, forgetting I had a new way to deal with them. It felt so natural. But once I write a poem and give it a title, the lesson it contains becomes more memorable. The poem is a monument to a particular change or revelation. I still had many relapses into depression, but often in those moments, a poem would come to mind. I would get that poem out, reread it, and get back on track sooner as a result.

Even as I write this, my progress sounds unbelievable. I am usually the first one to point out fallacies in logic or debunk beliefs without substance or scientific evidence. I like proof of validity. For two years, I practiced mindfulness meditation thinking to better deal with the mental tapes, stop the critical thoughts, and feel less stressed. It felt like prayer, where one never knows if God answers or any subsequent change in fate is just chance or coincidence. Near the end of those first two years, though, something amazing happened.

I found that training myself to be in the present, not thinking about the past or worrying about the future, cleared my mind. I was looking out the window at the storm, not caught in the middle of it. In this calmer, more rational place, I began to see, one by one, my faulty belief systems, destructive presuppositions, and also choices I never knew existed before. The meditation surprisingly revealed my subconscious' ability to heal itself. I have many flashes of insight and creativity while meditating. Maybe these had been there, and I had finally slowed down enough to notice.

Meditation also brought a new awareness of others. It troubled me how my own pain made me selfish and focused on my own problems. Through meditation, I began to see situations differently. I began to see new truths. When I described these to Brad, he often said a certain realization was a belief of Hinduism or Buddhism, or a theory of Jung or another psychologist. I knew the realization in question was also part of Christianity or Judaism. Amazingly, I was discovering universal truths, which many before me had discovered and integrated into religions or philosophies. Transpersonal psychology describes this as our spiritual identity. I was rising above subjectivity to the higher place of universal meanings. Growing my compassion and loving-kindness for others had the additional benefit of growing my compassion for myself as well.

Finally, an important aspect of my spiritual life is my religion. I have been a Christian since I was fourteen and always find strength and comfort from my relationship with God. For years, I watched Joel Osteen from Lakewood Church on television before I left for my own church service. When I moved back to Houston, I start attending there. Most weeks, the very thing I am working on is the subject of that week's sermon. It feels like I am getting extra assistance from God, and I appreciate Joel's sensitivity to bringing a timely message. During the hardest times, being able to participate in the worship with several hundred others and receiving an encouraging message felt like a critical element to making it through another week. Worshipping together with hundreds of others reveals universal truths and epiphanies.

A few months after finishing the poems for this book, I read David Richo's new book, *Being True to Life: Poetic Paths to Personal Growth*. It is about this process of using poetry in therapy, alongside mindfulness meditation, to resolve past issues. While I just stumbled into this process without much understanding of why it works, Richo describes the psychological, emotional, and spiritual basis for its effectiveness. He also offers many practical exercises for readers to learn how to do it for themselves. I recommend reading this book if you want to learn this process. He does a great job at breaking down the steps. He also teaches workshops based on many of his books.

## The Progression of the Book

This book chronicles three years in therapy with Brad Brager and meditation training with Micki Fine. I began writing as a way to make sense out of what was happening, with no intention of publishing or even sharing with anyone other than Brad and Micki.

Most of the poems are in chronological order. "A Life Emerging" is an overview. The poetry starts out identifying faulty thinking and counterproductive coping mechanisms. I was struggling with depression, feelings of helplessness, emotional withdrawal and isolation, and blindness to what was real. I had to reevaluate what I believed about God and the church. As I discovered mindfulness, there were many new realizations. I attended several full days of silent meditation and began to see the transformation begin which inspired; "Mindfulness" and "Spa Day." "Mariposa" was my first revelation of what I truly wanted to accomplish, a sort of blueprint for transformation based on the analogy of a butterfly's metamorphosis. It was also the poem where I found my voice.

I wish I could say my recovery was a steady incline out of depression, but there were many setbacks as problems in life brought back old habits. "Lead Me Back" was written when I realized how far I had slipped. But I was beginning to integrate more of what I learned, as I could hear Brad's and Micki's voices (in my mind) reminding me what I needed to do.

An event at work triggered what I later realized was a powerful *transference* back to a similar painful event that occurred when I was five years old. This remembrance was when Micki first taught me the process of befriending my past self to re-experience the event. It felt like a miracle. My subconscious began to bring back past events one by one, now that I had a way to resolve them.

When Valentine's Day approached in year three I wanted to write something positive about love, thus "Open to Love." I was at last having more good days than bad ones. I was remembering some of the things I valued about a loving relationship, and it reawakened in me a desire to pursue love again, even in current, damaged relationships.

One day a car ran over a woman, instantly killing her, in front of my office. The medical examiner could not come for hours, so her body lay in the street with a tarp over it for most of the day. I wondered how so many different events might have prevented this tragedy. She could have been delayed, or crossed at a different intersection. The driver could have come later, gotten there sooner, or paid more attention. This brought up memories of several auto-related deaths of people I had known, and my mother's death, for me to resolve (My mother locked herself in the garage with the car running). I saw that I had spent most of my life repressing and bottling up emotions so I would not have to deal with them. These feelings were beginning to leak out of the floodgates I built to hold them back.

My distant, depressed, unavailable mother always left me feeling motherless. As my healing progressed, especially going back and being a mother to myself, I began to replace the bad mother I remembered with a loving, internal one. There was empowerment in finding I no longer had to feel deprived, as I could mother myself.

"Voice Awakened" was a gift for Brad and Micki. I saw that their willingness to listen and care actually drew the poetry out of me. I do not believe I would have found my voice without sharing the poems with them and receiving so much encouragement and acceptance.

At another silent mindfulness retreat, while eating a peanut butter sandwich, I experienced for the first time some happy and nurturing memories of my mother, thus "Peanut Butter Memories." I was becoming whole. I had been grieving the loss of my mother since her death, and I decided to count the days. It had been exactly 15,998 days since her death, and I was finally coming to the end of my "16,000 Days" of grieving. This poem was one of the biggest monuments for me. Grieving was so much a part of who I was. In some ways, it felt like a part of me was dying to let that grief go. But I also felt like letting the grief go meant I would lose the only thing I had left of her. But letting go turned out to be less traumatic than I anticipated.

In "Self-Forgiveness," I began to forgive myself for all the stupid choices and mistakes I had made. I realized they had caused much of the depression and wasted years. I did not even realize how significant this act of self-forgiveness was until I felt the weight lifting.

As this phase ended, I wanted to paint a picture of the world I desired. It would be "A Universal Life" where all people realize that no matter how many ways we are different, there are so many more ways that we are the same. If we could focus on our commonality, while accepting and appreciating our diversity, we would all be so much happier. I have many friends and some family members who are gay and experience prejudice and bigotry from others in their family or community. Those who condemn or judge gay people justify their position by saying that homosexuality is a sin. My heart goes out to my homosexual friends and relatives, and I hope I have opportunities to speak up for them or help to make their way less painful. In many ways, we create a "Confined and Incomplete" life for ourselves when we could be free and fulfilled instead.

# Revelations

There were some life-changing revelations I found through therapy, meditation, and writing. Here are some of the most important ones.

*1. You do not have to wait for someone to "cure" you; it is completely within your own power to heal yourself.*

I believe in the value of a good therapist, but ultimately another person can never make you change. Being human themselves, they can also be wrong. Even the best advice will not change you unless you act upon it. Only you can make that decision to change. You have within yourself all the answers you need, if you can just learn to tap into them.

*2. Your healing does not depend on the actions of others. Even if they never change, it will not prevent your healing.*

In thinking about my trauma, I often thought that if others caused the damage, those others had to be a part of the recovery. I spent decades believing that if the people hurting me would change, then I would be happy. If they apologized, I could forgive them. Unfortunately, some of them are dead and others will never admit to how they injured me. It was liberating to realize that healing depends on our own choices. This also requires that you admit you may have also played a part in your own trauma: maybe not as a child, but certainly as an adult.

*3. Your happiness does not depend on circumstances changing. It only depends on the way you choose to view those circumstances.*

Even if you choose to stay in a relationship with someone who will not change, you can still change the way you respond to him or her. You can change how much you suffer, and you can establish new boundaries and standards for that relationship.

I hope you will pay attention to the poems that stir you emotionally, positively or negatively, as that is usually a good indication that it resonates with something in your subconscious. If you listen, you may be able to resolve past memories and find a life of wholeness, contentment, and happiness.

I finally accepted that even when I suffer, it is for my own good. The Bible says "we know that suffering produces perseverance; perseverance [produces] character; and character [produces] hope. And hope does not put us to shame . . ." (Romans 5:3-4). We do not always want to hear this, but suffering can be a positive force that drives us to change.

Mindfulness meditation teaches us to decrease our emotional reactivity by accepting everything, and also allows us to see the situation more clearly. Psychology teaches us that strong reactions are clues about something unresolved in our past and an opportunity to resolve them. It also teaches us that things that irritate or anger us are usually unmet needs. Therapy and meditation together have helped me find happiness and contentment, reduced stress and suffering, and a way to get my fundamental needs met, described as the "Five A's" by David Richo: acceptance, appreciation, allowing, affection, and attention (from *When the Past Is Present*).

# I

## Digging

# A Life Emerging

Looking back across years,
a strand unwinds slowly
as each life unfolds, trying
to reach the end intact,
without unwanted interruption,
without breaking too early.

Death tastes like honey
after a full life. Everything
experienced; laughter and tears,
celebrations, and never-again
lists made the hard way;
joy of babies born and
old lives gently returning
to the earth;
a natural course of
life cycles complete.

Strands begin the moment of birth,
traveling through time, disentangling
slowly, a destiny unfolding
every day, connected
to everything, everyone,
willingly or unwillingly,
all memories and their
emotions: Siamese twins,
sometimes needing separation.

Look back and listen,
vibrations of heart and soul,
reverberations of consequences
stretching back into darkness.
Who wants to go back
into blackest pain?
A human compulsion,
rubbernecking for trauma,
searching for blood and gore;
a moth spotting a flame,
urged on by primitive instincts,
uncontrollable, self-destructive,
but powerful still.

Searching for explanations to
restore a sense of purpose
with future reruns prevented,
avoiding that never-again list,
the burned hand wincing,
a warning of fire.
If only it really worked.

Instead, trudging forward in hope,
the tether tugs, sometimes yanks,
dragging attention backward.
Childhood revisited, blows relived,
where wounds never healed
and déjà vu never stops.
Hoping different outcomes
magically appear, but
everything has already happened
becoming hated history,
never to be rewritten.

How to dig up roots,
sources of turmoil; not band-aids,
covering never curing, only
weed-whacking tops of conscious
manifestations, letting them
grow back? Buried memories
returning, columbine and dandelion,
in life unwanted, spoiling
the garden's beauty.
The gardener's daily toil,
never-ending, sweaty struggles,
but worth the harvest.

Delicate seedlings contain power,
energy to move boulders,
break through concrete,
an unstoppable life force,
defying all containment.

Plants never stop growing,
buried but not really dead,
under junk piles discarded,
hidden and often forgotten;
life is determined to survive,
awaiting sunshine's glimmer,
patient for anyone
to clear away debris.
The crypt yawning open
revealing thriving growth.
Waking from slumber,
pale blades and stems,
starving for light,
finally spring forth,
surviving against all odds:
a life emerging.

## Old Friend

Old friend, gone so long.
Lethal, old friend,
want to take my life?
Something in me
wants to let you.
Normalcy still feels foreign
but you are my familiar,
life-long companion.
Prayer and meditation
take too much energy.
You are easy, exacting no effort.
Rivers beckon, no swimming there,
currents take over.
Everything floating downstream,
down into darkness,
deep into helplessness.
No effort, no work,
too exhausted to care.
You promise it will be easy.

Old friend, comfortable, old friend,
known so long.
Malevolent, old friend.
No matter how long apart,
it only takes a second
to reignite our relationship.
Have you been waiting?
New skills already forgotten,
months of progress reversed,
moorings coming loose,
undercurrents pulling down.

Old friend, addicting, old friend.
So warm, so enticing,
filling veins with deadly relief,
but at what price?
A life? My life?

# *Choices*

Helplessly, a circus horse
runs mindless circles, around
and around a ring, riders jumping
on and off; standing,
sitting, kneeling.
Just keep circling,
keep the same monotonous pace.
Don't slow down, don't speed up,
don't stop until told to do so
or whips refresh the memory.

Years of practice make the mind
an outsider, watching others
but seeing itself with eyes inside out.
Viewing outward appearances,
expert and cruel judgments, alone
against the world, always the loser.
Detecting flaws and magnifying them:
wrong size, wrong gender, just wrong,
inferior in every way.
A ruthless headmaster, standards of perfection,
rules to follow. Success is impossible,
failure is sure.

Seligman's dogs in a cage rigged for failure,
zapping volts. Can't stop the pain,
can't escape the pen until lessons are learned.
Nothing works, nothing changes.
No choices matter, suffering is inevitable.
The mind disconnects, pretends to be elsewhere,
giving away control.
The sooner the self dies, leaving only a shell,
a puppet with others, pulling the strings,
the sooner simplicity is restored.
The only choice left becomes
whether or not to live.
But there are always choices.
Some choose to remain helpless,
blaming others, easier than
taking responsibility.
Some seem empowered,
but the circus horse and caged dogs
never see that option.
What if the dog is too old to learn?

# The River

Standing on a riverbank
in the shade of an oak.
Arms fully loaded,
the soul collecting
unresolved relationships,
betrayals and regrets,
tormenting emotions:
self-criticism, self-hatred
all unbearably heavy
tumors on the soul,
deforming the heart
where no one sees
'til depression takes over.

Standing on that riverbank
remembering a promise.
Freedom comes by
casting thoughts, emotions
into watery currents
floating away.
Some resist, enmeshed with souls,
attachments still wanted,
purchased with suffering,
earning medals of honor
in trophy cases,
displaying an identity,
created with blood,
a value too high to give up
or let go.

Standing on this riverbank
choosing to believe the self,
not emotions. And definitely
not thoughts, just vaporous clouds
passing by. Sometimes stormy,
sometimes billowy,
but nothing tangible.
Reality is garbage floating by,
unwanted baggage, broken dreams,
remnants of relationships,
and the inability to move
or change.

Standing on my riverbank
with a focus on the breath,
letting go becomes the only option left.
Taking the grasping hand, slowly
unclenching fingers, forcing change,
the will battling the body,
the mind commanding muscles,
against their reactions,
throwing all into the river.

Heartbeat and breathing slow,
empty arms relaxing,
energy and strength returning,
depression diminished as
heart finds peace for a moment.

Now as firmly planted as a tree
by the river, ever ready to return,
to cast in sorrows and burdens
when they come.

# *Coats*

Self-protection is a thick winter coat
pulled tight with a belt.
Nothing gets in, nothing gets out.
Completely insulated,
everything trapped inside,
isolated and alone.
But is this safer, or just self-defeating?

Pockets filled with treasures,
souvenirs, mementos, photos,
some happy but many not.
Constant reminders of successes
and failures all trapped within
the clutched coat. The fool locking
the predator within.
No help gets through,
so the coat becomes a prison.

Hide all the wounds. Don't touch!
Don't come close.
The pain is unbearable,
festering and growing,
infections spreading.

There is always a choice:
keep doing what caused suffering,
or choose a healing pain,
stinging medicine dreaded
or surgery feared,
intense but only temporary,
offering a painless future.

# Blind

Born blind and unaware,
living in darkness. Unseen obstacles
hit and trip, hurt and trap.
Never seeing connections
or understanding all the ways
wounds reprogram the psyche
into self-destructive patterns.

Teenage introspection, translucent sight
of self-sufficiency. Hormones luring,
stumbling home in perpetual twilight,
never realizing what is missing.
Only those committed to
self-revelation hope to see
what is coming: a warning
to brace for collision, avoid
mistakes, soften blows,
enhance resilience or harden hearts.

Some find glasses: religion, psychology.
Focusing the vision but not increasing light.
Seems clearer, distance closer, but limited.
Seeing only expected, acceptable explanations,
conformity, believing one side only.
Rose-colored glasses or shades.

Some find the truth sought.
After dead ends, a window opens
making the endless night vanish.
But sudden brightness, stabbing retinas,
forces eyes to squint.
A life now seen in iridescent color:
Dorothy waking up in Oz.
Confidence crumbles,
foundations unravel,
some truth becomes lies, and
some lies have more truth.

Deep sadness, grief pouring down
for all the years lost in blindness,
never knowing every relationship
was based on midnight's unreality.
Problems looked black, though really
blue and green. Moments of happiness
seemed sad gray, only foolishness,
the eyesight painting them gray
and responding accordingly.

Everything changes in daylight,
looking bleaker from loss.
Tears flow, though resisted.
Wrongs blamed on others, self-inflicted.
Despair takes over, beliefs are questioned.
No solid ground to stand on,
to start from or to build on.
Everything changing at once.
Heart racing, life frozen in fear.
Too much chaos.

Have to move forward. Which direction?
Time to reevaluate. Where to start?
Time to think. What is truth?
How to organize what's left?
Understanding needed to restore order.
Strength needed to rebuild.
Insight needed to see new reality
in the bright glare of sunlight,
to face the new season.

# Where Is God?

An identity intertwined with religious teachings,
hard to distinguish reality from indoctrination.
Time to discover heartfelt beliefs, values.
Time to get rid of oppressive ideas,
planted by zealots, controlling and selfish,
imposing agendas, taking away
individual freedoms.
Thwarting desires to hear God's voice,
spoken directly: the still, small voice,
unique words of comfort and love,
filling heart voids, keeping faith alive.
But how can the soul distinguish lessons
from doctrines?

The damaged, needy soul absorbs religion,
reinterprets, filters through lenses
of the past, creates fear
in the present and future,
needs attachments to those
offering acceptance,
a place to call home.
Swallows destructive ideas,
internalizes, incorporates into
heart and soul. Chooses to become
indoctrinated.

Fear of harm and danger
assuaged by group protection.
Confusion of a stolen childhood
rests in peace of certainty found
in communal dogma and rituals.
Longing for love; a magnetic attraction
to canons, traditions, devotion to creeds
so perfectly matched in expectation;
a glove fitting onto a hand.

The inner orphan searches for spiritual family,
the pastor or priest becoming the father
every soul desires. Lives deprived
of parental love become attached
to anyone willing to fill the role,
making bonds to churches powerful
through the energy of transference.
Hard to remain objective,
forgetting no person or group is perfect,
none have all truth and wisdom.

In this complementary union,
the child within can't stop
from regressing
back to the role of dependence,
unquestioning trust. Trying to satisfy
the longing, stop the aching.
Accepting all as normal and healthy.
A primary relationship's bond,
so critical for survival, never challenged.
Objectivity and discernment
turned off by belonging
until some point like now,
when new trauma obliterates
once-secure foundations, forcing
self-discovery to start,
separating truth from fabrication.

# II

# *The Breath*

# In This Moment

The storm is here
once again. Swirling thoughts
confuse the mind.
Emotions become a vortex,
sucking everything down
into the pit.
This is too familiar,
but I am more prepared this time,
armed with mindfulness
to see the truth, and let it be,
in this moment.

Beware your eyes.
Deceptions filter sight,
disguising reality.
Just a pair of glasses to change.
Through transparent lenses
the situation is teacher,
the lesson is wisdom,
surrendering to processes unfolding.
Glad to be fully awake
observing suffering and shadow,
wounded heart, growing compassion.
Willing to say yes
in this moment.

Beware your thoughts.
All is illusion
Openly received, but not believed,
let all thoughts stay or go
in this moment.

Beware your emotions.
Though acute, they are
just smoke and mirrors,
never held or pushed away.
Feel pain and pleasure fully.
When gone, no harm is done
in this moment.

Finally living in present moments,
finding contentment in what is,
finding peace in having
an open hand,
grateful to be alive
in this moment.

# Wake Up

When tightness is felt
in heart or head,
wake up. It's just a dream.
When pulse races,
urging flight,
wake up, it's not real.
When fear rises,
soul disappearing,
wake up, stand up tall!

So much goodness,
peace, and kindness.
All are thirsty, drink it in.
It's a choice to stay right here,
in this place, in this moment.
Why let mind and emotions
drag away the heart?
Wake up and stay!

When the mind is falling,
darkness closing in,
wake up and see the light.
When ready to give up,
future seems too bleak,
wake up and look around.
When the world closes in,
limiting choices, vision, hope,
wake up and expand!

There is much joy
and loving-kindness.
All are searching, take it freely.
It's a choice to stop right here
in this place, in this moment.
Why let suffering rob, imprison?
Wake up and live!
There is much space
and contentment.
All want freedom. Turn the key.
It's a choice to stay right here
in this place, in this moment.
Why carry burdens? Let them go.
Wake up and breathe!
Just breathe.

# *Mindfulness*

In a room full of people,
find solitude and warmth.
In a whole day of silence,
find an ear to hear *Yes!*
All eyes close in darkness.
A distant light
brings hope, peace,
and loving-kindness to all.

Close the eyes, find the breath,
listen to the body.
Find the breath once again
notice sounds.
With the breath as anchor,
look up to the sky.
See all the clouds?
They are thoughts floating by.

# Spa Day

A spa for the soul,
where life is paused
for a short time,
and every concern,
problem, or worry
left outside the door.
They may still be there
when the day is over,
but just maybe,
some will not.

Everyone comes
with spots and stains
where life collided
with attempts to succeed
at work, at home,
with others and self.
Living is messy,
most experiences, mixtures
of wisdom and ignorance,
are a series of first-time events,
with no manual.
Times of flow alternate
with times of struggle,
leaving the soul to carry
the burden of consequences.

Today, an opportunity
for cleansing the soul.
A room full of people
all unique individuals.
Each receives something needed
to remove blemishes and
for a short time, is able to bask
in the peaceful present,
letting all that comes
be just what it is.

So bathe in spacious awareness,
everything and everyone connected,
no judgments or expectations,
much gentleness and acceptance.
Life is good.
Why do so many miss out?

Unless one has a receiver,
radio waves can fill a room
yet remain unheard.
Compassion fills the room
and the universe.
Just need to slow down,
tune in and listen,
allow love to heal,
to wash away roughness,
bringing ease and comfort,
and finally discovering:
happiness need not be
a rare event.
It is available to all.

So turning to the breath.
with openness to
whatever each day brings,
the soul is purified, refreshed
to resume life's challenges
once again.

# III

## Mariposa

# Death

In this darkness of death,
in this stillness of loss,
is a detour from life.
Driven by urges unknown,
propelled by repulsions and desires,
an actor in somebody's play.
But there is always free will,
though it never seemed so then.

Encased in this self-made shroud,
all else crowded out of sight;
a sensory deprivation tomb.
Not knowing how long waiting lasts
or if it will ever end.
A first experience
with no chance to practice first.

Looking back to the sequence of events,
to a mixture of blindness and truth.
Could mistakes have been prevented?
Were there forks in the road?
Were warning signs missed?

Now all paths converge
on this final, engulfing event.
Time cannot be rewound,
so just let it play.
Now wait and listen to the silence.
Wait for a glimmer of light.
In the waiting,
learn to breathe.
For death is not the end,
it is just the beginning.

# Letting Go

In this timelessness of in-between,
where a minute is a day
and a year is just a blink,
the waiting feels eternal.
Initial impatience fades,
omnipresence diffusing
into the void.
Impulses to do
screech to a halt
in the compression of the capsule.
Resistance is futile,
the only movement the breath.
All that remains
is to *be* without doing.
Time to be self-sustaining,
releasing stores of treasure within;
the soul's reserve,
weighed and measured.
All that was gathered
better be enough.
Life or death is in the balance.

Can love and happiness be found within?
Can the receiver also be the giver,
or will it feel like a cheap substitute?
Will dreams be lost forever?
Did the losses die in vain?
The price of the future is
paid for with suffering.

But it's not just final destinations
that matter. The journey,
filled with obstacles and setbacks,
is a personal trainer for life.
A blueprint of hope
drawn long ago,
details carefully chosen.
Time to throw it out, start again.
No more plans or expectations.
New designs developing.

Now wait
for the signal to wake up.
Wait for this process to end.
Remember:
no one knows the future,
it has not yet been written.
So in the waiting,
find and savor
the present moments.

# *Positive Core*

As death turns to decay
in this final decomposition,
all life ends up the same.
Dust to dust.
The earth reclaims its elements,
ready to recycle.
Birth, life, death, and rebirth
circle eternally.

Universes made of a few hundred atoms,
but infinite numbers of configurations.
Limitless possibilities and potential ahead.
Bonding, reacting, destroying, creating.
All seek completion in perfect balance,
to settle into wholeness,
filled with contentment and peace.
A positive core surrounded
by a negative shell,
with a neutral *now* holding
everything in its place.

Good and evil, tension
between polar opposites.
Light and darkness, needing
contrast to be seen.
Happiness and sadness
together a bittersweet medicine.
Where is the positive core of man?
Is it in the soul or the spirit?

From the devastation
of a million past sorrows,
the heart becomes a lump of coal:
dark, cold, fragile.
Enduring pressures within and without,
through the storms weathered and beaten,
with every fall or failure
a new resolve to stand again;
a stripping away of old beliefs;
questioning, searching, and
sifting out the lies.
Only truth remains.

Hanging precariously by a thread.
Vulnerable to everything
but fully awake,
the eyes refocus and watch.
Fear turns to peace, releasing control.
Remorse to self-forgiveness
and anger to loving-kindness.
A revelation unfolds
that everything has a purpose
in the right season.
That life's tapestry is
filled with colors and patterns,
but the full picture
is never appreciated
until it is finished.

Destiny waits patiently for fulfillment,
unchanged by wrong turns, dead ends.
The emerging new life
adjusts each path,
weaves each thread so they return
to the True Path eventually.
So wait without fear of tomorrow,
accepting some things are unknowable.
Wait in the peaceful assurance
that no one is ever alone
while resting safely within
the Father's loving hands.
In the waiting,
learn to live now.

# *Transformations*

A metamorphosis of the heart,
where time is not measured
and the final creation
has no resemblance
to its former self.
A caterpillar enters the chrysalis,
molecules disassemble
and reassemble anew.
The butterfly emerges,
a new creation.
Carbon-black and dull
buried in the earth
'til future discovery finds
a diamond clear and bright,
reflecting light in all directions.
Volatile atoms
dangerous and reactive,
capable of mass destruction,
finally finding a perfect match
in one, two, or many others.
Though each alone was unfulfilled,
community brings stability.

A dead life, a heart of coal,
is finally laid to rest,
surrendered and content.
No more regret or anxiety,
no more asking how far.
Just remembering moments
when grace finished bridges
when love provided shelter
and protection,
when meditation's gift
was a moment's moratorium
from war.
When compassion shared
the weight of the burden,
when comfort tended
to the wounds,
and when faith granted
the ability to see one's best self
in the eyes of another.

As screaming thoughts are silenced,
the moment's experience freezes
into a snapshot.
As free as a butterfly newly hatched,
the mind has no boundaries.
The heart transforms into a diamond,
strong enough for a new foundation.
Light creates life with energy released
as each dawn brings a fresh beginning,
watching the neutrality of the present
become the past memory,
good or bad.

Through acceptance the only outcome
is a heartfelt appreciation for one's
fully awakened humanity.
No one is promised a perfect life.
Life is not fair, nor assistance a given,
but regardless of wisdom or mistakes,
all finish in their own time,
their own way.
Each scar is a reminder of a past victory.
There was injury but also healing
and strengthening.
Now wait, with breathless anticipation,
for each new sunrise.
Wait until the tapestry is finished,
when the final breath whispers,
*It is good.*
In the waiting,
live now in the happiness
of a boundless heart.

# IV

# Changing

# Turning

Muscles tensing, fingers gripping,
speed picking up, white water ahead.
A waterfall plunging, disappearing
into clouds of spray, obscuring final impacts.
A rollercoaster with no tracks.
The worst part, anticipation of the unknown.
Where will the body wash up?
Too much turbulence,
a life dragged along against its will
reacting to crises but never quite prepared.

Rivers driven by circumstances,
sometimes torrents. Numbness setting in,
then bitter winds blow off course,
trying to capsize; distractions to trap
in preoccupation.
Other times, scorching sun
burns away joy and hope, leaving
only emptiness, erasing happy memories.
With years of practice, running on inertia,
guaranteeing no deviation.
How can a negative force become positive?

Peace is not an absence of trouble.
It's the assurance that hurdles should be jumped,
increasing strength and stamina
for each new challenge.
Knowing the race will be run and finished
but on one's own terms.

Joy is not an absence of sorrow
but the ability to accept life givens,
knowing after every winter comes spring,
and what looked dead is only sleeping,
waiting for the right moment
to spring forth with new life.
Love is not an absence of pain;
it is confidence that bonds will hold
through the fiercest storms
of hurt, disappointment, betrayals.
Knowing each remains open and giving
with no expectation of return.

Time to find old dreams once lost
and dust them off. Protecting
new dreams just blooming,
turning the river by dropping a boulder
right in the middle.
Just say no to old habits, choices.
With every boulder, resistance provides
the option to turn aside.
Begin a new path,
a safer, more peaceful way.

As siphoning begins,
creating its own force,
momentum keeps it going
as a new pathway begins.
Feel it flow into a new life.

# Lead Me Back

Lead me back where I started.
It seems so far away.
I can no longer see it,
and don't know the way.
A voice showers gently
cools and quenches the mind,
gentle words like an arbor,
sanctuary of vines.
It sounds like your voice.
Lead me back.

Lead me back to reality.
Wake me up from this dream.
It feels more like a nightmare,
and I can't seem to breathe.
Lead me back to the present.
The past can't be changed.
The future's still waiting,
shrouded and strange.
I remember your voice.
Lead me back.

Lead me back into spaciousness,
'cause I'm locked in my cell.
I can feel the compression
once again in my hell.
Lead me back to contentment.
All I feel is regret
for mistakes I have made,
for the traps I have set.
I must follow your voice.
Lead me back.

Lead me back to the solitude.
Only me and God
hush the critical voices
that make my head throb.
Lead me back to the breath.
I'm distracted again,
falling into the darkness
with my suffering and pain.
I will follow your voice.
Lead me back.

Lead me back into mindfulness.
Don't know how I strayed.
I'm lost in a desert,
burning sun and no shade.
Lead me back to my river.
Lead me back to my tree,
where my thoughts and emotions
can't hold me, where I'm free.
I am following your voice.
Lead me back.

# Time Against Time

Some say time is a line
that starts at birth
and ends at death.
Some think it's a ray
moving into eternity,
with a momentary transition
from physical to spiritual.

The body participates fully
in linear time but begs
to go back:
to correct stupid mistakes,
to prevent destructive words,
take better care of body, soul, and heart.
Always impossible, futile to wish,
because time is the master,
all else is its slave.

Another kind of time
passes in the mind.
No linear boundaries or rules,
just a spoiled child
going wherever she wants,
not caring who gets hurt.
Replaying the most painful
moments of the past,
maintaining pain indefinitely.
Traveling in circles
away from the present,
a giant figure eight
going back to the past
and then into the future.
No matter how much one wants
to stop the rollercoaster,
to stand still in the present,
to get on a train
moving slowly in one direction,
forget about it.
The past never left behind,
the future never left alone.
Constant distractions derail the mind,
triggering a memory.
The mind time-travels
against the will.
It knows the way so well.

Mind and body travelling
in two separate times,
forever joined in life but
forced to play by different rules.
Envying each other,
never in sync
or the same dimension.
Each forever destined
to want what the other has,
never to exchange places
or find peace.

Where is contentment
when trapped
where you don't belong?

# Without Love

An unloved child begins
a life of pain and rejection
not knowing why.
An unwanted child grows up
with fear of abandonment,
no ground to stand on.
Expecting all to disappear,
worthlessness confirmed,
being thrown away
or sent to live elsewhere,
becoming someone else's
problem, like trash.

A battered child
makes a fist early.
Always in enemy territory,
constantly vigilant
for unexpected attacks,
barricading bedroom doors,
hoping to stop the predators
in the family.
Sleeping with one eye open,
trusting no one.
Believe nothing until proven.
Most of all, hide the heart
from humiliation and shame.
The child slowly starves,
but nobody notices.

No matter the passing years
or the adult each becomes,
inner children live forever,
emotionally frozen, forever alone,
trapped in Neverland, motherless,
and never able to move on
or grow up.

# Childish Games

A tug-of-war raging.
Two wills and agendas,
two worldviews.
Each grips the rope tightly,
clinging to habits.
The ways to win:
have the strongest arm,
the most tenacious resolve,
or the sharpest tongue.
Winning is everything.

In between a chasm,
dropping into darkness.
No one knows what lies below
until too late.
Why are the only outcomes win or lose?
Only one winner and
always one loser.

Both are losers
when winning costs a relationship.
For now, unhappy but connected,
then one wins, the loser falls,
and the relationship dies.

Combatants of equal strength
create a stalemate. No one moves,
each waiting for the other to weaken,
an exercise in futility.
If no one wins, why play?
A tic-tac-toe lesson in revenge,
no longer about winning, only preventing,
so the game becomes lose-lose.

What would happen if just one
stops playing, releases the rope,
stops coercing, allows change,
starts over, agrees to disagree,
and begins to face reality?
It may not be worth saving.
The other will falter, unbalanced.
Fall down and wake up,
grow up and change.
Childish games left behind
for a saner, more humane home.

Bridges, built for connecting
two who are separate, distinct.
One builds to the other or
both build to the middle.
Either way, choices to build and
choices to cross reveal anything
left of value.
Time to face change
and face the consequences.

# V

## Triage

# Save the Child

A lost child is finally found,
but not by the parents
who could not love her,
who did not want her,
or appreciate all that she was,
but by the mother
she became.
After raising her own children
with the love, compassion, respect
she never knew,
she could go back
across time and space
to the small child
with sadness in her eyes
and the hesitant smile.
To those moments when
she cried out for love
but none was given.
She can send wishes of love
and acceptance to the child,
knowing exactly what she
always longed to hear.

*May you feel loved in every cell of your body.*
*May you feel valued and appreciated for just who you are.*

She can go to those moments
when the child felt endangered
by those who should have protected,
who made the ground shift
beneath her,
so she lost her balance and confidence
and never felt safe again.
She could reassure her,
knowing what the child
could not know:
she always had the strength
to protect herself alone.
There would be suffering
but she would make it,
becoming stronger.
Now tell her:

*May you feel safe and protected from harm.*
*May you feel secure, knowing you have all you need already.*

When old memories, old wounds
become freshly painful, triggered
by a thought, a smell, a feeling,
the actions of family or friend,
she can look back
to find their origins.
She can locate that child
at whatever age,
in that moment long ago,
when she felt she was a mistake,
or too assertive, too needy,
too unacceptable in every way.
When she searched for
acceptance and validation,
and tell her:

*May you feel wanted, valued, and cherished.*
*May you know that your life is a blessing, not a curse.*
*May you know that all your gifts will one day bless yourself and others.*

The child's family
was blinded by selfishness.
Though they used
anger and humiliation
to belittle her offerings,
rejected to coerce her
into submission and helplessness,
though they made her feel
unlovable and alone,
she can now go to her,
put arms around her,
give her hugs she never felt,
show her how to keep their words
from piercing her heart
by not believing them.
How to ignore their barbs
and accept that they
may never really see her,
and that someday others would.
She can send a wish
for the child:

*May you be at peace in the midst of life's storms.*
*May you be happy and free.*

As each wound is healed,
as tears dry up,
may she leave the past,
focusing all her attention
on the present, becoming
all she is meant to be:
building new relationships
to give and receive love,
relaxing and
letting go of fear,
sleeping restfully
dreaming sweetly
of sunshine
instead of only shadows.
For the first time
she will feel whole.

# Thanksgiving

Give thanks for breath,
a fundamental requirement for life.
Silent bonds connecting all beings
throughout all time.
Plants and animals
exchanging breath,
diffusing and connecting
in the atmosphere:
a perfect symbiotic relationship.
Compassion felt for fragility of life,
how it ends in minutes
when the breath stops.
So give thanks
for each breath today.

Give thanks for choices,
be they focusing on what's lacking
or grateful for all one already has.
When opportunity knocks,
the door opens wide.
All that is there received
like a gift from a friend,
not overlooked as insignificant.
This thought counted,
filled with love and kindness
which no one can ever
have too much of.
So give thanks
for the ability to choose wisely.

Give thanks for things
that *can* be controlled.
As thoughts are tamed, they change actions.
When actions change, new habits develop.
With new habits comes strength of character.
Stronger character produces patience,
persistence, and strength.
Through patience, hope is renewed.
Through persistence, dreams come true.
Through strength, difficulty turns to ease,
leading to increased wisdom
and better control of the thoughts.
So give thanks
for controlling so much through so little.

Give thanks for situations
that always pass.
No matter how painful,
no matter how pleasurable,
all ends eventually.
From the ashes of a life or dream
emerges the new beginning.
Never too late to begin
something new, as
each sunrise starts a new day
filled with possibilities.
So give thanks
for an ever-changing world.

Give thanks for all the things
that increase when given away.
Help offered to others becomes
karma in return, sowing and reaping.
Love from one, joined with another,
grows exponentially, a life overflowing.
The more one offers compassion
to all beings, the more it returns
to the sender, connected to all.
Becoming a good friend brings
friendship in return,
increasing joy and peace.
So give thanks
for a bounty of eternal virtues.

Give thanks for the breath,
a focal point in meditation, offering
a break from life.
With a relaxed, rational mind,
choices and insights, not yet habit,
challenges are manageable,
new truths revealed.
Feeling connected to all.
The quiet joy of appreciating
all that is beautiful.
Comfortable just being oneself.
So give thanks
for the simplicity of the breath.

A breath.
So easy, all are able,
child or genius,
none prevented from receiving
all the breath can bring. For this
everyone can give thanks.

# The First Brick

A stronghold in the mind
needs to be conquered,
though not through force
or strength of will,
but by finding its foundation:
that event or situation
long ago, when the first brick
was laid during time of weakness.
A choice made, maybe for no reason,
maybe from childish ignorance,
helped the stronghold stay.

A lightning flash of memory
of a moment long ago shows
a hurting child alone in her room.
Banished for disobedience,
ordered to do the impossible.
Obedience means overwhelming
shame and embarrassment,
but disobedience brings more
rejection and isolation.
So she chooses to disobey;
the only option possible, knowing
her pain will only get worse.
She is more of an outcast
in her own family.
Another opportunity to help her
so she knows she is not alone,
in this fight.

No one dared go this far before.
None could face the wrath of father
and stand their ground.
All had crumbled in his
oppressive, violent presence.
All knees buckled under his force.
The child knew that feeling well.
But he claimed, the choice was hers,
never thinking she would defy him.

From the outside it looks
like a battle of wills, and
she is winning.
None knew how she felt trapped.
If there was a way
to choose otherwise, she would.
But fear of shame was too powerful,
strong as a wall, blocking her retreat.
So she stood there, looking defiant,
but she was really fighting for her life
with her back against that wall
as the first brick was laid
in the stronghold of depression.

So tragic how the first brick
was chosen by a four-year-old
who didn't know another way,
or how devastating and crippling
these choices would be
to her entire life.
Parents became enemies,
now needing protection from them,
starting her isolation. Her new solitary
confinement is her home.
Eventually solitude becomes
a permanent shroud, hiding her
preventing any reprieve of her sentence.

Hard to see the bars of prisons
you make yourself until too late.
Helplessness saps
energy needed to change.
Hopelessness convinces there is
no use in trying, nothing works.
So you continue to build
brick upon brick,
as depression deepens,
becoming a way of life.

Go and tell her the truth
kept from her:
no one is ever alone.
Go and calm her storms, with arms
of protection and love.
Bring her a sledgehammer
to smash each brick of
self-hatred and despair.
Go and bring her the maul
to demolish her walls.
Tell her who she truly is,
a child of the Most High God:

*May you see your visions come to be.*
*May you know your radiant true nature.*

# Empty Façades

Façades of relationships mask missing depths.
Instead of secure roots, established foundations,
only raging undercurrents hide and wait,
pulling everything apart when given a chance.
Nothing feels right, nothing seems real.
Shallow pleasantries exchanged by two people
living together and apart.

The bullfighter and the bull
purposely avoid real contact,
putting on a show, pretending to meet,
only illusions and misdirection.
The bullfighter taunts the bull,
the cape invites for a dance, but
when the bull closes, bullfighter dodges,
never allowing connection.

Bullfights start with picadors, not deadly,
just meant to weaken by bleeding.
Pretending to have a relationship,
but really an enemy, willing to kill.
Constant struggle increases blood loss.
Arguing may stop, but days of silence
create more distance, more resentment.
The bullfighter then uses his sword
to finish the task, and the relationship ends.

Two people never connecting,
two languages, same words
but different meanings.
What does love really mean?
Personalities are contrary:
what one loves, the other hates,
each one's needs forever unfulfilled.

An eternal broken record,
same arguments, same pain.
Numbed by the chill of avoidance,
the relationship freezes,
each expecting the worst of the other.
A demilitarized zone, a false sense of peace
trapped in the fog of no man's land.

Is beauty found in the unlovely,
looking past horns and swords,
to see treasures of the heart?
Can the family be saved?

# VI

*Love*

# *Again*

## Reactions

Never the initiator, never in control.
After the impact of another force,
any response reveals attitudes, feelings,
often prompting opposing actions.
Choices made from anger or hurt
change one fundamentally.
Two volatile chemicals change one another,
so nothing is ever the same.
Filled with regret and wishing
for better solutions. In the meantime,
learn to resist them.

## Resistance

A self-protective act
like slamming on brakes to avoid a crash
or choosing not to give in
to everything, increasing suffering.
Problems arise when resisting good things
becomes a lifestyle.
Can anyone really learn to be accepting
without natural defenses engaging, interfering?
There must be a way to stop resistance
and to stop the resentment
it eventually creates.

## Resentment

Feelings buried without resolution,
anger caged, growing and festering,
not believing anyone could be
so cold. Demanding perfection,
unreasonable requirements for love.
Consider only two alternatives; conformity
and death of the true self,
or remain true to self
and kill the relationship.

## Reconsider

The current reality is unlivable,
offering no choice.
Consider a new reality
where prison cell
becomes a garden,
offering refreshment and serenity,
a moment to reflect on the gap
between the present
and a desired future.

## Reflection

A time to assess the countenance
staring back from the mirror
of life's choices.
Do eyes reflect happiness and peace
or sadness and turmoil?
Is sadness unwanted or unacceptable?
Find out how to change.
Imagine how happiness looks
so it is recognized
when it arrives.

## Recognition

Finally understanding something clearly;
accepting its validity,
realizing the futility of continuing
on the same dark path.
Can a broken life feel whole?
Or is it just one more time
to give in or give up,
let others off the hook
in the name of peace,
trading in old beliefs
for justifications.
Or is it really resigning?
Settling for second, third best?

## Resignation

Accepting the inevitable, but
with a negative spin.
After years of struggle,
living miserable and frustrated,
can relationships really change,
when it feels like something
is lost or taken away,
like letting the bully win?
Hard to let offenses go
especially without assurances
that bonds will be re-created,
reborn as a good life.

## Re-creation

Created again, better this time,
a complete makeover or synthesis.
Drawing blueprints for reinventing.
There has to be a vision
before any plans begin
or the end will not look right,
like building a house and
forgetting the foundation.
But where are visions found?

# *Eternal Voices*

Mother,
lost in death so long ago,
is rediscovered alive and well
inside the dark mind,
where the inner child
has carefully preserved
every memento, memory;
cataloguing images remembered,
preserving recordings of a voice,
the mother's voice.
Words filled with intonations
never needing interpretation,
always knowing their meanings.
That voice, those words
heard year after year,
branded onto the psyche,
trying to control the child
long since grown.

A voice never challenged,
the self-subordinated
to its unwavering authority.
Emotions firmly established
in early years when survival
depended on saving
a primary relationship,
internalizing voice so completely.
No longer two, but one.

Most live thinking
decisions are theirs,
destiny depends on choices
solely, when all along,
like a puppet master,
the mother's voice
silently directs all:
mind, emotions, and actions.

Sometimes the voice is a good mother.
Others times a bad mother.
But either way,
the heart still clings.
A voice so important, any
sacrifice just to maintain,
either for survival
or a belief that without mother
life is over.
For a child
left with only a father,
survival is a clear concern.
Can't survive *without* his support,
can't survive *with* the sociopath
he becomes. No amount of resistance
prevents the father's voice
from integrating itself into
the mother's voice within:
still micromanaging.

Internalization automatic,
feeling so natural, like being home,
validating lies that "unlovable" means
no real choices.
The unlovable are really beggars,
after all: holding out cups
hoping for pity, for someone to drop in
a little love or acceptance.
Deserving nothing, receiving little.
And the worst part: settling
for beggar's crumbs,
without any options, until now.

Time to disconnect the voices—
alien parasites, separate,
unwelcome. All the worst parts
of the mother, depressed, detached,
unable to reach beyond her pain
to nurture her children.
And the father, angry predator
hunting the vulnerable, breaking
the will to fulfill selfish dominance.
And the selfish lover, only wanting
some clay to mold something new,
rather than loving who is already there.

Can that voice of comfort and guidance
be the self's own voice, becoming
its own mother?

# *Limping*

There will always be a limp.
The broken heart is patched together
but never truly whole.
When life puts rocks on the path
or gouges out potholes,
slow down and step carefully.
Wounds injured again
bleed easily, just like the first time,
complete with original pain.

Accept limitations.
Be alert for obstacles of rejection,
emotional unavailability,
broken promises, and cruel words.
Never let them cripple again.

Gratitude felt for feet to walk with
when things could be worse.
Still walking miles ahead
of the blind with their canes.

# Open to Love

Standing on a precipice,
a crossroads with a choice.
One direction leads to safety.
Everything exactly in its place,
predictable, comfortable,
neat and tidy, but closed.

The other direction
into unknown territory.
Pulses racing, passions flaring,
volatile emotions getting loose,
carried away by love's abandon.
Stumbling around in the dark.
Messy and imperfect, yet prized
above all else. And love has to be
chosen every single day
all over again.

Love holds the marionette strings
of each heart it captures,
making normal, rational people
willing to be fools:
to leap without looking
headlong into the hope that
this might be *The One,*
the soul mate who knows
deep secrets of the heart.
Acknowledgment of risks:
That an exposed heart
can be broken, wounded deeply,
maybe beyond repair.
But no regrets in suffering,
as glimpses of paradise
makes the heart yearn forever.
Open eyes to wonders of love.
Once tasted, once experienced,
there is no going back. Hold on tight,
give up everything, for its priceless reward.

One of life's inevitable challenges:
acknowledging all are born alone,
die alone, with the in-betweens
searching for connections.
Sharing love, life, and dreams
with limitless possibilities.
Sharing sorrow, disappointment,
realizing all of it is a part
of being fully human.

When life leads to the edge
and, looking down the cliff,
death feels certain, remember
the antidote for fear of falling
is to jump instead.
Dive into love with arms
flung wide, ready to embrace
everything.
Live each moment fully.
After it passes, it is gone.
Face the future
with eyes alert, focused,
appreciating life's full beauty,
made of light and darkness.
Complementing one another,
times of struggle and ease,
knowing none appreciate
pain's purposes or how love
weaves two lives together.
In the end, only bonds
strong enough to outlast time
are valuable above all else.
They are bonds of love.

No matter how frightening,
stay open to love.
Breaking up is hard, but
stay open to love again,
when least expected,
even if everything inside
screams it won't. Persevere
so it is recognized, received.
So tragic to miss it
with heart closed and hardened.

Today can be the first step.
Standing on this precipice,
at a crossroads with a choice,
everything is simpler;
choose love.

# VII

## Convergences

# Strongholds

How many seconds in a lifetime?
How many split seconds?
Intersections of multiple lives,
multiple events, coming together
at a moment's convergence.

Separate paths in life,
long chains of events,
never a pause or lapse in time,
just ticking off the seconds left.
Seconds never noticed
by lives mindlessly doing
the same thing
day after day, wasting
all that precious time.
Lost in thoughts of the past,
future plans. A body on
autopilot. Actions done
a thousand times before,
don't have to think
until startled by
something catching the eye.
Hopefully it won't be too late
to prevent a tragedy.
So much can happen
in just a split second.

In a split second the newborn
takes its first breath to live.
In a split second
a thousand thoughts become
a flash of insight.
In a split second
a decision or failure to decide
can lead to a tragic death.

# Triggers

Just as the mind is jolted
suddenly into the present,
hoping whatever just happened
is not a terrible mistake.
So many lives changed, families
destroyed, hearts broken,
lives forever connected
by convergences of calamities.

Others arrive on the scene;
bystanders passing by
or gawkers. Few resist
the attraction of the drama
and later regret the images trapped.
Too close this time
to simply ignore.

Even at a safe distance,
even with eyes shielded,
there is powerful déjà vu,
a devastating familiarity to
something from the past,
the soul unbalanced.
A very thin line between
being an observer and
an unwilling participant.

Three earlier crashes.
Deaths remembered.
Three cars, three deaths, three traumas,
and now a fourth bringing
it all back.
Each with the same aftermath.
Powerful flashbacks jump
into the eyesight unexpectedly.
The mind hunting for possible
alternate scenarios where
just a split second sooner
or a split second later,
a moment's interruption or delay
would prevent death.

Feeling finality, the overloaded mind
shuts down.
The soul feels hollow, empty,
like it left or went dormant.
Any minute it should change back
but doesn't.
Waiting for feelings to return,
waiting to feel alive.
How long will it take this time?
Is this how shock feels?

# Release

A deep sorrow felt
as memories resurface.
Emptiness floods from the past,
vague memories and
the worst memory of all:
The shock of sudden death
completely devastating,
a life already over
before anyone noticed.

The mind rejects the obvious:
no reasons to explain,
no one to blame.
Sometimes death just happens.
A chains of events converges
at just the right moment,
and reactions occur.
No matter how hard
the mind searches
to find a window or door
when an intervention
might prevent death,
there isn't much use. Because
tragedy already happened and
struggle tortures the mind.
If only this, if only that.
If only.

Then the soul begins
to take responsibility for
not doing something.
So the pain of loss increases,
the guilt grows stronger.
Regretting words unspoken,
all the love withheld or
taken for granted,
wishing there was a way
to apologize.

Now time freezes everything
until resolutions are found:
the dead child's bedroom enshrined.
The mind doesn't know
there is never satisfaction
or resolutions.
A hamster on a wheel
running in circles,
thinking it's getting closer, but
only running into futility,
never noticing how
unexpressed grief solidifies
into a mental roadblock
preventing all attempts
to move on.

In this stalemate, between
reality and hope,
peace and contentment are found
by letting go
and then waiting.

# *Resurrection*

A doorway leads down
into vaults of the mind,
to unresolved traumas.
Once too painful to process,
once thought irreparable,
now changing.
A necessary spring cleaning,
to dig up and cremate the past,
leave a tombstone marking its place,
a reminder of finished business.
The key: the similar experience,
though not traumatic,
just enough alike to trigger
all the memories.
Then the real work begins.

Nothing like a powerful transference
to jog everything loose,
resurrecting skeletons
to rise and float to the surface,
no longer forgotten.
Sometimes only the subconscious
knows what is happening,
how to find a path home.

All begins with a convergence.
Survival techniques learned in childhood
to deal with abuse are now maladaptive,
deal with stress by denying emotions,
avoiding persistence to capture
the attention. Stress builds up
in ulcers and headaches,
insomnia and depression.
The suppressed mind
tries to communicate
the only way it knows.

A convergence starts the chain reaction,
triggering hidden explosives,
becoming a catalyst for
a soul set free,
a final acceptance,
a resolution of grief, all
locked up by the hurting child
now set free
by the healing adult.

All lives and events converged
now continue on their own trajectories,
becoming a divergence of blessing.

# VIII

## Opening

## Broken

A body damaged, no longer whole,
seeking something or someone
to lead the way
or at least indicate
a general direction to follow
for rehabilitation.
Sudden losses pierce,
with stark contrast to
how things were better before.
Compulsions to fix brokenness,
restore functions; as before,
a picture of desired results
still burned into memories
as the motivator.

But damage and loss
developed over time
may remain unnoticed.
Subconscious slowly adapts
to minor changes not worth noting.
Frogs in a pot of cold water
slowly boil to their doom,
never attempting to escape, their
cold-bloodedness slowly adapting.
No alarms or warnings,
so no action taken,
life speeding to its end,
going the wrong way
and going too fast.

A mind abused and misinformed
assumes the present reality
is the only one possible.
Little seeds of lies,
beliefs planted early
before self-awareness filters,
drilled in and watered,
grow into thorny weeds.
Bad decisions, regardless of intent,
share the same consequences.

A broken body may be permanent,
but broken minds may not.
Some are restored to health
or close enough to find
happiness and peace.
Puzzling how division
between voices
keeps some, not others,
brings wholeness,
like cutting out cancer
making the body whole,
a subtraction being an addition.

# Floodgates

A barrier discovered deep in the soul,
emotions imprisoned behind floodgates,
safely contained, or so it is thought.
The soul hopes to avoid the heart breaking,
the life crushed, or relationships dying.

Emotions only bring agonizing affirmations.
Rejections are deserved, permanent and real,
both far too painful.
Years of tears never cried
become oceans of sadness never expressed,
grief never processed. What goes in
never comes out.

Many life-altering decisions are made in trauma,
emotions carried away, tears never ending.
Trying to restore equilibrium by turning them off.
But few understand how another soul feels.
After a while, forgetting the grief
of another's loss. Compassion dries up,
leaving only impatience; an expectation
it should be over. But the soul left behind
cannot comprehend why the whole life
has turned to rubble, with no instructions
for putting it back together.
Can't stay in pain, can't move ahead
when the life is broken.

A puzzle always missing the last key pieces.
So either from exhaustion or frustration
the terrible feelings are closed behind
gates sealed shut, until someday,
when life is easier.
Emotions leave, replaced by cold numbness,
easier to bear, and harder to stop.
So years tick by as gates remained closed,
eventually forgotten.

In time the mind justifies hiding
all the feelings, the soft spots
where one sharp stab
starts the bleeding again.
Better to hide vulnerabilities,
stay constantly vigilant, keep gates locked.
But rumblings are heard, the dam is breaking.
Hinges creak, tears spill over.
Better to open before it all bursts.
But where is the key?

# *Hiding*

The life others see, so small and incomplete,
the tip of the iceberg, hiding much more below,
concealing evidence of trauma.
The soul, fragile and brittle, a fall leaf crumbling,
projects competence, an image for others.
Only a matter of time before falling apart.
An incongruity between self and the mask,
with truth wanting to prevail.

Time to let truth emerge, no longer avoiding
fearful thoughts and emotions, at peace with the shadow
without becoming ensnared.

Feelings jump and shift, instant tears go unexplained,
triggered unconsciously by invisible connections
watching without, reacting or hiding.
What are they saying?
Where is the key?

# Opening Slowly

A heart shut tight by the twelve-year-old self
terrified by emotions too powerful to feel.
Punched in the gut by a sudden suicide,
face to face with suspicions of neglect,
abandonment, by a mother's rejection.
Love is withheld, or was never there.
Attempts to win love and nurturing
were useless and at an ending.

Floodgates hide overwhelming emotions,
locking everything up, but soon
forgotten, until decades later.
A random death causes déjà vu.
Transference reveals powerful emotions
are finally ready to be addressed.

The mother's voice, identified and separate,
removing regret, and erasing guilt,
images fabricated from pieces of memories
filled in with wishes of impossible perfection.
The heart's constant search for her substitute stops.
Floodgates are overdue to open.
Memories wanted and unwanted come,
allowed and addressed as each passes through
the gates at last.

# IX

## Mother

# Compassion Within

Monstrous emotions
overwhelm again,
triggered by events
forgotten for decades
but clearly just waiting.
The mind's connections
between now and then
expose emotional nerves,
jolting life to a stop,
transporting bottled-up,
forgotten emotions
into the present.

Transference is recognized by
reactions too strong,
too extreme and devastating.
Let the inner child speak.
Finally someone helps
the compassionate mother within,
giving back the stolen voice
silenced by suffering,
to help her free
the heart imprisoned.

# Abandonment

Seven months since
a mother's death.
Summer breaks
and father's plans.
Banishment to grandma's,
a farm far away.
Sounds like a fairy tale
but not with her,
a bitter woman,
cruel and abusive
always believed
before the child.
A tortuous summer
trapped in a nightmare
and no amount of protest
changes his mind.

A first plane ride alone.
First time gone for weeks.
To another child
in another situation, exciting.
But to one withdrawn,
this is sitting on death row
waiting for the inevitable end.
A deep sadness felt
for garbage unwanted.
Just one more in a series
of uncontrollable events
changing the life forever.

The hours and days
count down,
fill with boredom.
Time creeps.
The one comfort is a horse,
a friend without demands,
just feeding and grooming
in silence.

The hardest time is bedtime.
Activities ceased with
no more distractions leaves
the mind remembering.
Suicide changed everything.
Re-asking the unanswerable,
hoping repetition will bring
different answers.
Why did she do it?
Why no warning?
Why did no one stop her?
Why did she never imagine
her impact on others?
Why she didn't love
enough to stay,
or make other choices?
Trying to understand
but the heart never does.

Silently, controlling tears
bring exhaustion by day.
So when darkness comes,
alone and upstairs,
in a old creaky farmhouse
with too many bedrooms
a thousand miles from home,
the tears saved up
are silently released
into pillows with care.
No one hears,
no one knows.
Hopefully renewing strength
to get through
the next day.

Finally returning, but not
really home,
a black-sheep status
confirmed by becoming
invisible.
A birthday forgotten,
not the last one of childhood.
Excluded from fun,
an outsider inside
her own family.
Fears confirmed, with
paralyzing implications:
An inanimate object
inhabits her bedroom.

Nightmares start
always the same:
coming home to
family gone,
moved out,
no forwarding address.
Only things left behind:
abandonment, rejection,
loneliness, and fear,
permanently taking up residence
in the soul.

Without the mother,
the secure anchor vanishes.
The child flounders
searching for connections,
looking for breadcrumbs
to find the way home.
No arm reaches out
pulling to safety.

Is a surrogate family
a figment of the imagination?
Does belonging come
from anything real,
or is it just one-sided attachment
like a child and her blanket?
The orphaned child calls
for love and belonging,
wanting to come in
from the cold.
But is anyone out there?

# Home

Can longing be satisfied
by any kind of love?
Or does love have to match
the hole in the heart?
The mind invents scenarios.
The loss felt strongest
becomes the obsession.
If mother's love withheld,
only mother's love restores.

If true, then every orphan
is doomed, never to feel loved.
Or the heart can open
to all kinds of love:
friends, children, teachers
even a pet,
or strangers sending love
into the universe.
And if nothing else,
self-love is always available.
What matters most is believing.

All carry mother and father
inside, loving unconditionally
a loyal friend, comforter, and refuge.
No perfect people
or perfect relationships.
No perfect love. So give up
Hollywood fantasies with
*happily ever afters;*
perfect soul mates,
one-and-only fits.
Just unreality.
End eternal searching,
learn once again
to trust and connect?

The compassionate mother within
opens the door,
inviting orphans in.
The voices of missing mothers
are found in the hearts
of grown-up children.

# Peanut Butter Memories

The simplest things
become doorways, unlocking
memories long buried,
suddenly returning with vividness.
The mind remembers
sadness and pain best.
The worst events,
just so many to choose.
Happy memories hide
beneath, waiting
for a smell to call them back.

A busy week, no time to shop
leaves little to use for the sack lunch
on a day of meditation.
Some things always around
like a jar of peanut butter
in the pantry, never spoiling.
Add a little jelly
and here is a sandwich,
easily transported,
awaiting the mindful lunch,
never suspecting
its importance.

With a first smell, the mind transports
back to the kitchen table,
where as a child, seven years
of meals were eaten,
many peanut butter sandwiches
on white bread, cut into rectangles—
never triangles—
the crusts removed.

There were other sandwiches
at that yellow linoleum table
with benches on two sides,
a large window at the end.
Bologna sandwiches,
egg salad,
tuna fish.
On special days, Hawaiian Punch
instead of milk.

One rainy day, boredom sets in.
Wishing for coloring books
but too poor to buy one.
Mother says to color
napkins. All the embossed flowers,
leaves, and borders look
absolutely impossible
until she sits down
at the kitchen table to show
her coloring proficiency,
an amazement to all.

Other kitchen memories appear:
breakfasts of pancakes and bacon,
fried chicken dinners with
lemon meringue pie.
Sourdough starter under the sink,
sometimes overflowing if ignored.
Coming home from school
finding mom sitting with her best friend
Betty, drinking Postum or cocoa.
Both laughing and never running out
of things to talk about.
So talkative, so full of life.

Other days, finding no mother home
but knowing she is laughing
in Betty's kitchen,
a sharp contrast to
her future.

Surprised by her happiness
forgotten.
Happy moments existed,
free from depression,
before she was stolen
from all by a suicide.
For now she is happy,
playing with her children
on a rainy day.

The lingering emotion: wonder.
Wonder and awe
and gratitude for
unexpected blessing,
never planned but
always hoped for—a miracle
happening today.
A first-time remembrance
of the good mother,
the happy mother,
making the soul feel like a
missing part has returned,
life a little bit closer
to being whole.

# 16,000 Days

Forty-three years plus ten months:
time passed since tragedy,
a death vitally connected
to the heart.
A death unexpected.
No time to prepare
or prevent regrets, speak
unspoken words
of reconciliation.
A death so tragic,
choosing suicide over life,
telling loved ones "not enough,
not worth staying."
The juvenile self, incapable
of processing all that will change
with her selfish decision, and
consequences still paid
by all the family anyway.

An arrogant father commands
children never to speak
of her again,
subverting healing.
Never ask questions;
no when, how, why.
Never experience natural
stages of grief.
Just bottle it up, repress it
bury it, and watch it slowly
devour the soul.
Not enough time for learning to cope,
so the 16,000 days of grieving
start ticking.

Might have lasted forever
except for synchronicity,
beginning in the last thousand days.
A convergence of circumstances and lives
bringing together the right people
at just the right time,
when the soul is ready and open,
or desperate enough to try anything.
The right people to help
without pushing, guide
without controlling,
and restore hope.

Changes begin slowly at first,
gentle shifts in thinking, reprogramming reactions,
mental loops stopping, beliefs retooled,
unlearning helplessness, finding power in choice.
Internal storms seen clearly
as illusions no longer resisted,
watched from a distance, no engaging,
eventually disappearing.
Lies fade with truth replacing.
The work done,
ghosts cross over, unfinished
business completes.
The self is no longer alone,
no longer haunted.

Each memory is a teacher,
each event an opportunity
to go back and rewrite history,
applying adult perspectives.
Strength found in wholeness,
inner child and outer adult.
Contentment filled,
forgiveness given, mercy received,
grateful for grace.

Grief can be brief or never-ending,
over time forgetting what
its absence felt like.
A micro-focus hiding progress,
obscuring time's passage,
causing amnesia for anything
different from sadness or abandonment,
until a peanut butter memory
filled with love
recalls a happy past,
and a flicker of light
signals the coming dawn,
the first new morning
in 16,000 days.

So pack away black clothing.
Raise the half-mast flag.
Bury the paper cranes
along with the grieving identity.
Bereavement has finished.

# X

# Revival

# Excavations

Defenses peeled away, each new layer reveals
another part of the story.
An archeological dig into the soul
discovers the history hidden
in artifacts buried deep in mental strata.
Broken pieces of evidence help to explain
delusional thoughts and behaviors
so natural, so normal, but distorted.

A worldview seen through abuse and trauma,
products of faulty upbringing, but also
choices and habits.
This ongoing expedition into the subconscious,
powered by a hope that truth is discovered
and revealed, makes finding life's meaning
easier.

Each fragment unearthed is studied carefully,
an inference made about original use.
Maybe a bowl or pot for feeding,
or a painful reminder of how many times
it was empty, the heart starving,
wishing there was food in that bowl
but not knowing how to get any.
Eventually there is no need for
empty bowls. They are thrown away,
eventually buried, forgotten.
But lessons are branded on the soul,
so every relationship looks just like
that empty bowl, the heart refusing
to pick it up. If accepted,
there will be expectations of being filled
with love and compassion,
and if not, all the pain, rejection
will return.

Each artifact comes in its own time,
with truth calling. Something resembling
a crude weapon, maybe for protection
or maybe to hunt, or build a fire
to keep away cold.
Postures and attitudes ensure distance,
building shelters of self-protection,
angry walls between relationships.

Artifacts once useful to a frightened child—
behaviors and responses, reactionary and destructive
—provided a hiding place, a safe refuge.
But the child is now grown,
and what worked then, doesn't work
now, because everything changed
except the child.

Strange how different parts of the self
grow up at different rates, or not at all.
The body has no choice:
birth, childhood, adulthood, old age, and death.

Emotions have their own lives,
maturing at different rates:
the childish, irresponsible adult,
the teen wise beyond their years,
the child raising younger siblings,
sometimes stagnating, and other times
breaking speed limits.

The mind is omnipresent. Past, present, and future
all become one, sometimes forgetting
where thoughts come from.
Hard to know which voice speaks:
the child, teenager, or someone else.
The future, the wishful thinker, fatalist.
But only the present mind changes a life,
cultivates, and strengthens it.

Relics discovered, dug up, examined
are processed, resolved.
The archeologist reassembles history
to uncover truth.
Willing to explore the fear provoked,
addressing associations, choosing fresh looks
through present reality. No longer a child,
no longer dependent.
The adult has nothing to lose
except the dead weight of suffering,
and everything to gain: possibilities of happiness,
hopes for wholeness and connection.

Dirt and blood washed away, relics are
now seen as treasures, gold within
making the soul stronger.
Struggles become coach and trainer,
journeys become more important
than end results.
Excavations of the unconscious
clean out cancers and restore vigor.
The journey doesn't end until death,
unifying self and soul
and reassembling the life.

# Voice Awakened

A question: Is a sound real
if never heard by another?
Do trees falling in forests unheard
become silent noises?
Can a voice live if no one hears?
Or will it just disappear?
Do thoughts and ideas
trapped in the mind
have meaning or substance?

Vibrations use connections
to bounce off molecules
in all directions at once;
a rippling effect, like a stone
dropped into water,
until all energy is spent.
Sounds in space's void,
having no connections,
silenced and immobile,
are never heard, meaningless.

Can a voice silenced by neglect
reawaken when called by
encouragement, appreciation?
A rebirth starting with baby steps
of verse. First words coaxed,
arms outstretched, ready to catch.
Wobbly and uncertain toddling,
valued for innate origins,
words no else could speak.
If nurtured and strengthened,
each poem leads to the next.
Never knowing what lies ahead
as line leads to line, creation unfolds.
Somehow believing,
it will be freedom
filled with hope.

Insight dawns: Words construct
the path to follow. A treasure map leads
to the buried prize. A scavenger hunt
collects all the pieces of a life
and reassembles them.
Poems unlock the prison
setting free from solitary,
silent confinement, building a structure
where futures turn from darkness to sunlight
and fogbanks lift, revealing
the way of truth.

Words now spoken aloud,
sound waves rippling,
confident skipping and running
down trails of experience,
reveal heart wisdom.
At first drawn out but now
heard by the self, significance
felt and understood, revealing
secrets buried, training the soul
to live the new life.

The crippled self-transformed,
now running the race to win,
owes all to the willing ear,
attentive to newborn voice
without judgment or criticism.
The poet's voice reveals
a breadcrumb trail leading
out of dark forests,
finding a way home.
The attentive self
provided energy to start
momentum, siphoning,
as flow begins,
now self-perpetuating.

Trees in forests
no longer need another to listen.
The tree hears itself changing,
making that sound
real and true.
Now free to speak, creating
vibrations to the universe,
words needing to be heard,
transforming lives.

# *Passing Storms*

Sitting in meditation, peaceful solitude,
by a window, looking out, seeing nature,
wild and chaotic, sometimes dangerous.
Blue skies turn cloudy, gray to black.
Impending storms cannot be stopped
only weathered, inside or out.
Nothing prevents the clouds from filling
with rain or choosing where it falls.
Storms have no prejudice, coming to all
eventually, never singling out,
though it sometimes feels that way.
Just waiting until heaviness demands
a release.

Clouds and storms superimposed
over beautiful blue skies, removing
bright, sunny feelings, replacing
with sadness, foreboding, disappointment,
never knowing the worst of the storm,
only the inevitableness
of its coming.

When circumstances can't be controlled,
better to practice patient acceptance
with palms upraised, surrendered
to the experience, what it teaches
where it cleanses the soul.
Washing away debris no longer needed
a bathing that sorts priorities,
opens eyes to new truth. So wait
for storms to pass—they always do—
and learn.

Watching storms build, trees bend and bow
to nature's power. The papery leaves,
so fragile, hold on tenaciously
to life as winds try to scatter.

Suddenly appearing in the middle
of the darkest cloud, a small hole reveals
blue skies behind storm's mask,
a glimpse of what lays ahead,
making waiting more bearable
as hope is renewed.

Muted grays and dark diffusion
give way to bright white.
Storm clouds become soft billows,
new fluffiness seen against blue skies,
once again bright and sunny.
Trees resume their erect presence,
leaves glisten brighter
shiny from showers removing grime,
leaving all better off.
The heart understands in open willingness.
It is cleansed too, and unharmed.
A deeper appreciation felt, for the storm
and blue skies.

# In the Stillness

In the stillness of meditation,
focus on breath alone.
Problems and worries cease,
stresses and work are laid aside.
In this moment
only one concern:
to take a breath and
breathe it out again.

In the stillness of thoughts
all life is frozen.
Careening scripts pause,
removed from drama.
In this moment,
chaos settles into order.
Only one thing matters:
the next breath.

In the stillness of the emotions,
screaming voices are muted,
sometimes dark and stormy.
But soon blue skies return.
In this moment,
drama no longer exists.
In the waiting,
learn to breathe.

In the stillness of the heart,
the whole universe is felt,
breathing in unison,
feeling love, happiness, and freedom.
In this moment,
all have much in common,
breathing out
compassion to all.

In the stillness of the soul,
find perfect solitude,
just an automatic rhythm
of body, mind, spirit.
In this moment,
restore importance
found in the simplicity
of the breath.

In the stillness of the life
after years of hard work,
changes become natural.
No more effort or struggle.
In this moment,
filled with ease,
harmony becomes
as natural as the breath

In the stillness of this moment
filled with universal love,
limits are removed,
doors opened to happy futures.
In this moment,
all you have to do
is welcome everything
and breathe.

# Self-Forgiveness

Compassion flows freely
to an inner child
so vulnerable, helpless
in family decisions,
or abuse from parents.
No compassion though, for
the former adult self,
the person whose choices
lead to years of suffering.

Remembered as weak,
stupid, and afraid,
brainwashed by religion
allowing bullies to rule,
never protecting the self
or standing up. Afraid
of rejection, labeled a *jezebel*,
wanting to belong too much,
wanting love too much,
wanting secure protection,
but never getting any.

Relationships start out
promising, but end up
with holes in their umbrella,
letting life rain down,
soaking the broken heart.
Umbrellas for one leave
others in the storm, no protection,
no real connection.

Convinced that love means
pleasing others, trying to become
what is wanted, expected.
Hide the true self, bury it,
and in the end, kill the self.
All are required to be someone else
when the real self is unwanted.
Only reproof felt now for
the younger self; should have
known better, should have
left earlier. Warning signs were clear
but ignored. Signs were posted;
ulcers were a sign, and
deepening depression.
Betrayal is a clear sign.

No mercy for her helplessness,
no grace for her reasons,
as no reasons justifies staying
under those conditions.
Now the heart must find
something deserving compassion,
any reason for mercy.

Feeling concern requires seeing
and remembering what life was like.
Searching for her face
in the mind's vault, an image comes.
Standing in the kitchen
with her newborn son, firstborn,
wearing the blue dress she hated.
The only thing fitting now,
but a symbol of oppression.
Coerced to buy, painful to remember
but more painful to wear.
A choice to avoid conflict,
to endure ridicule to keep the peace.

Now remembered, eyes full of fear:
fear of rejection and failure,
abandonment. Deciding to be strong,
a lifetime of self-protection, no one
sharing the burden. Danger everywhere,
no one willing to help
or bothering to ask or see.
The hope for acceptance
fading more each day,
a series of disappointments,
déjà vu from childhood.

Her face, anxiety etched,
dark sorrow in her eyes,
a resolve to be someone else
or to die trying.
The brainwashing slowly killing,
replacing with a mask
to hide the hollowness
growing inside.

Seeing her loneliness
feeling her still-broken heart,
mercy felt for choices.
Time to go to her with
a heart of compassion,
becoming the mother
she never had.
She was the same age then
as beloved children now,
making all easier.
Time to become the arms of love
she never felt.
Time to forgive.

Standing with her face to face,
taking two hands in two hands
not sure what to say.
Speaking with gentleness,
the elder tells the younger:

*May you feel loved in every cell of your body.*

Words speak the deepest desires,
eyes overflow with tears.
Attempting to hold them back
even if the only other witness
is she.
Ashamed for being a baby,
a lifetime bottled up,
protecting the heart from cruelty.
The mother tells the daughter:

*May you feel safe and protected from harm.*

Unexpectedly, knees buckle.
Crumpling to the floor, dazed.
Realizing suddenly the heart longed
for those words never heard:
now there is someone
offering protection.
A final gift of loving-kindness,
words the heart remembers missing:

*May you know you are beautiful just as you are.*

Silent tears turn to deep, shaking sobs.
Something deep inside breaks open,
a flood releasing pressure
never before recognized.
No more words needed,
just two versions
of the same person
sitting on the floor together;
the older holding the younger,
a mother holding herself
in love and compassion,
in safety and protection,
in total, unconditional acceptance,
but most of all in forgiveness,
as more lost pieces return
to complete the soul.

# XI

## *Universal*

# *Confined and Incomplete*

Carefully trained since childhood
on the importance of judgment:
right from wrong, good from bad
or sometimes evil.
Creating prejudice toward difference,
because different is wrong and bad.

Convinced of an afterlife: heaven or hell,
and nothing in between.
Superiority in believing truth
belongs to only one elite group
with membership restricted.
A truth made of rigid rules:
*God's laws.* Narrow doctrines,
limited personal definitions,
severe, merciless prerequisites
for entrance into heaven.
Callously condemning others to
eternity in hell, or so thought
by those blinded.

But small-mindedness bred in ignorance
only brings hell's punishment now.
That which must be avoided, *Hell,*
is invited in instead.
Explanations hide truth,
justifications create validity,
lies brainwash the unsuspecting
into embracing a lifetime of horrors—
holy wars and holocausts—
by promising a reward
of eternity in heaven.

Entrance fees paid in full
by self-proclaimed martyrs, believing
"pay now, reap later." Beware,
any slip-up not rectified quickly
with devout and fervent repentance
means unexpected death will seal fate,
directing the soul straight to hell
for a moment's transgression.

Indoctrination completed
by invoking God's name as author
of the madness, ensuring none
challenge or try to disprove.
But the true deception:
Dogma forces all to focus on futures,
an unverifiable afterlife, forgetting
to live now. Best to be unaware
of an unwanted life chosen,
with all the treasures missed;
an end-justifies-the-means mentality
works so much better.

Choices made to harm go unnoticed
and unfelt, the life never lived
only endured or tolerated,
sometimes thrown away, worthless.
Death becomes the desired
pathway of escape from sorrow,
becoming the inspiration of spirituals:
Crowns of glory, mansions in paradise
heavenly home, swing low sweet chariot,
coming to take me home.

The exiled longing for heaven,
the mind exchanging reality of this life
for hope of an afterlife, filled with
constant joy and eternal rest.
A promise: no suffering or pain.
Though it only exists in imaginations.
Reality becomes unreality,
fabrications become the preferred reality,
though really delusional thinking.

# Despoiled

Innocent bystanders fall prey
to hatred and cruelty for being different,
unable or unwilling to conform,
powerless to change race or color,
gender preferences. Reluctant to change
religion or culture, or deny the true self,
to become a false representation of
what others want.

Kidnapping Native American children
for indoctrination in state institutions,
missionaries in foreign countries
demanding conversion to Western ideals,
and raping the cultures.
Homosexuals deprogrammed, treated as criminal.
The overweight told they wear their sin
for all to be disgusted,
an obvious lack of discipline.
Attitudes of the ignorant,
who attempt to control or coerce,
berate or humiliate, force into regimens:
a trail of tears, love in action, a size-ist society.
Just to alleviate their own prejudice
of having a relationship with someone so
repulsive, embarrassing, unacceptable.

Adding up the ways people vary:
By race, creed, color,
religion or beliefs,
sexual orientation or desire.
The sum total is a mere fraction
of the ways that all humans
throughout time are exactly alike.
No one turns down an organ donated
or asks about its former owner's race.
All pales in importance compared to
things that truly matter:
loving-kindness, acceptance, respect,
family, giving, helping one another,
empowerment, success,
compassion, and goodwill.

Yet cruelty is easily defended
by those misled by righteous resolve,
forcing compliance with selfish agendas,
removing the shame or need for excuses,
preventing the death of expectations
of carefully planned futures, held on to
tenaciously by gripping fingers.

If only all could see
the universal value of five A's:
*Appreciation* for all, regardless
of understanding or believing.
*Allowing* diversity with respect
and expressions of compassion.
*Acknowledging* innate worth.
*Attention*: carefully listening
to show that the heart cares.
*Affection*: Love and belonging
relationships feel like home.
All speak clearer than words
as priorities fall into place.
People are more important
than doctrine or personal preference.
Be willing to seek a better life,
the universal life.

# A Universal Life

The heart longs for a universal life,
all journeys and destinies, combinations
of finished and unfinished work,
learning and growing,
being both novice and expert,
everything allowed to be
just where it is, never ending.

The soul longs for a compassionate life,
transcending pettiness,
seeing over walls built by fear,
looking beyond the superficial.
Sharing resources,
goodwill that perceives beneath
defensive armor the best in others,
embracing loving-kindness from others
and from self; never earned or bought,
only freely given and received
by open and receptive hearts.

The life longs for a universal world
where divergences from norms
unite to build community filled
with connections, where the blind
receive their sight, and wars end.
A universal world filled with
universal love and joy
forever.

# *Stand Up*

A new page turned, the next chapter begins,
a fork in the road, offering new paths,
a new door opens, revealing springtime,
the long, dark winter past,
hope bursting forth uncontained.

Just when the heart almost gave up,
all options tried and failed,
middle age signaling inevitable decline.
Prime over, never recaptured,
opportunities missed, gone forever.
Just when all was lost, a new life started
free from depression, empowered and energized,
the mind calmed and peaceful, the past resolved
through subconscious leadings
and deepening gratitude for blessings
no longer hidden or ignored.

A deep appreciation for milestones of poetry:
truths revealed, lessons learned, new habits begun.
Unwholesome mind-states discovered, diminished.
Healthy ones strengthened, creating more.
Each poem commemorating
timely and much-needed assistance,
a constant reminder for all passersby:
it is never too late, life isn't over 'til death.
In the meantime, there is always hope.
The soul sings again, a song of revolution,
a song of declaration, of synthesis, happiness,
creativity and flow:

Stand up, stand up tall,
no more hiding in the shadows,
proclaim out to all
who you are with honesty.

Stand up, stand up straight,
with self-confidence and honor
knowing you have all it takes
to live your life in dignity.

Stand up, stand up free,
with all those willing to join you,
who believe in the best that you can be.
Don't let anyone define you.

Stand up, stand up strong,
with all your sisters and brothers,
where you know that you belong:
drawing strength from one another.

Stand up, stand up for
all who follow your example.
Pave the way so many more
can find their freedom, hope, and peace.

Stand up, stand up proud
for all you have accomplished.
Celebrate and sing out loud.
You have earned victory!

# GLOSSARY

**Automatic cognitive-affective spirals:** The habitual thoughts and emotions which lead to a series of thoughts increasing in severity: e.g., Someone says something mean. You think they are mad at you. You tell yourself it is because you deserve it, and the relationship ends, all your relationships end this way, and you will never have a lasting relationship. In reality, the person might be having a bad day and their comment has nothing to do with you.

**Cognitive narrative experience:** The things we tell ourselves about ourselves and interpreting the meanings of experiences.

**Mindfulness meditation:** The practice of present moment awareness and a focus on the breath in order to keep the thoughts, emotions, and body sensations from controlling us.

**Post-partum depression:** Depression commonly seen in women after the birth of a child.

**Schema:** The categories we create in our mind to simplify information we learn.

**Shadow:** The term used by Carl Jung to describe the part of the unconscious mind that represents unwanted weaknesses, instincts, beliefs, behaviors, and abilities often repressed and denied: the subject of *Shadow Dance* by David Richo.

**Transference:** The projection of unconscious contents and the basis of relationships. We tend to "replay the past, especially when our past includes emotional pain or disappointment" and then we "cast new people in the roles of key people, such as our parents," from *When the Past Is Present* by David Richo. Someone dislikes a person who reminds him or her of a disliked parent or sibling.

# RESOURCES

William Brad Brager, MA, LPC
815 Walker St. Suite T14
Houston, TX 77002
(713) 318-4788

Micki Fine, MEd, LPC
3701 Kirby Dr., Suite 890
Houston, TX 77098
www.livingmindfully.org

Jung Center
Houston, TX
www.junghouston.org

Jon Kabat-Zinn
Center for Mindfulness in Medicine, Healthcare, and Society
www.umassmed.edu/cfm/home/index.aspx

Joel Osteen Ministries
www.joelosteen.com

David Richo
www.davericho.com

Spirit Rock Meditation Center
www.spiritrock.org
Woodacre, CA 94973

# BIBLIOGRAPHY

Csikszentmihalyi, Mihalyi. *Creativity: Flow and the Psychology of Discovery and Invention*. New York: Harper Collins, 1996.

Chodron, Pema. *Start Where You Are: A Guide to Compassionate Living*. Boston: Shambhala Press, 1994.

Goldstein, Joseph. *Insight Meditation: The Practice of Freedom*. Boston: Shambhala Press, 1994.

Horney, Karen. *Our Inner Conflicts: A Constructive Theory of Neurosis*. New York: W.W. Norton, 1972.

Kabat-Zinn, Jon. *Full Catastrophe Living: Using the Wisdom of Your Body and Mind to Face Stress, Pain and Illness*. 15th Anniv. ed. New York: Random House, 1990.

Kabat-Zinn, Jon. *Wherever You Go There You Are*. New York: Hyperion, 1994.

Klein, Charles. *How to Forgive When You Can't Forget*. New York: Liebling Press, 1995.

Nhat Hanh, Thich. *Reconciliation: Healing the Inner Child*. Berkeley: Parallax Press, 2010.

Richo, David. *Shadow Dance: Liberating the Power and Creativity of Your Dark Side*. Boston: Shambhala Press, 1999.

Richo, David. *The Power of Coincidence: How Life Shows Us What We Need to Know*. Boston: Shambhala Press, 2007.

Richo, David. *When the Past Is Present: Healing the Emotional Wounds that Sabotage our Relationships.* Boston: Shambhala Press, 2008.

Richo, David. *Being True to Life: Poetic Paths to Personal Growth.* Boston: Shambhala Press, 2009.

Rubin, Theodore. I. *Compassion and Self-Hate: An Alternative to Despair.* New York: Simon & Schuster, 1975.

Salzberg, Sharon. *Loving Kindness: The Revolutionary Art of Happiness.* Boston: Shambhala Press, 2002.

Seligman, Martin E. P. *Helplessness: On Depression, Development, and Death.* San Francisco: W.H. Freeman, 1975.

Seligman, Martin E. P. *Learned Optimism: How to Change Your Mind and Your Life.* New York: Free Press, 1990.

Williams, Mark, Teasdale, John, Segal, Zindel, and Kabat-Zinn, Jon. *The Mindful Way through Depression: Freeing Yourself from Chronic Unhappiness.* New York: Guilford Press, 2007.